David Luff Prc
presen

C000030651

Herding
Cats

by Lucinda Coxon

Herding Cats was first presented at the Ustinov Studio,
Theatre Royal Bath, on 7th December 2010.

The play was subsequently presented with the same cast
by David Luff at the Michael Frayn Space, Hampstead Theatre, London,
on 6th December 2011.

Herding
Cats

by Lucinda Coxon

cast (in order of appearance)

JUSTINE	**Olivia Hallinan**
MICHAEL	**Philip McGinley**
SADDO	**David Michaels**

creative team

Director	**Anthony Banks**
Designer	**Garance Marneur**
Lighting Designer	**James Mackenzie**
Composer and Sound Designer	**Alex Baranowski**
Costume Advisor	**Susan Kulkarni**
Production Manager	**Lloyd Thomas**
Stage Manager	**Katy Munroe Farlie**
Photography	**Simon Annand**
Associate Producer	**Mark Cartwright**
Producer	**David Luff**

Production Acknowledgements

Andrew Smaje, Amie Shilan, Charlotte Wilkinson, Sarah Dickenson, Patrick Brennan, Siwan Morris, Oliver Millingham, Paul Owens, the Stage One Producers' Bursary, The Pineapple Kentish Town.

cast

Olivia Hallinan | Justine

Theatre credits include: *Precious Little Talent* (Trafalgar Studios); *Listen to the Wind* (King's Head Theatre); *Macbeth* (English Shakespeare Company); *The Famous Five* (King's Head Theatre and UK No.1 tour); *A Midsummer Night's Dream* (Cannizaro Park); and *Psychosis* (John Thaw Theatre, Manchester). Most recently, Olivia starred as Laura Timmins in the hugely popular *Lark Rise to Candleford* (BBC, series 1-4). For her leading role as Kim, in the critically acclaimed BAFTA nominated *Sugar Rush* (Channel 4, series 1 and 2) Olivia received an International Emmy Award (2007). Other television and film credits include: *Jack Falls* (Press On Features); *A Risk Worth Taking* (Lead Gate Productions); *Chickens* (Channel 4); *Girls In Love* (Lead – two series, Granada Television); *The Bill, Murder in Suburbia, Trial and Retribution* (ITV); *Anything's Possible* (Hat Trick Productions); and for the BBC Jimmy McGovern's *Moving On, Casualty, Just William, Torchwood, Holby City* and *My Family*.

Philip McGinley | Michael

Theatre credits include: *Hobson's Choice* (Sheffield Crucible); *Canary* (Liverpool Everyman/Hampstead); *More Light* (Arcola); *The Changeling* (Cheek By Jowl); *Great Expectations* (RSC) and *Kes* (Royal Exchange, Manchester). Television credits include: *The Gemma Factor, Casualty, Battlefield Britain, Hawking, The Deputy, Dalziel and Pascoe* (BBC); Tom Kerrigan in *Coronation Street, The Bill, Cold Blood, Heartbeat, Blue Murder* and *Falling* (ITV).

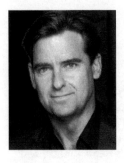

David Michaels | Saddo

Theatre credits include: *The Constant Wife* and *Death and the Maiden* (Salisbury Playhouse); *Tactical Questioning, Hutton Inquiry – Justifying War, Called to Account* and *The War Next Door* (Tricycle); *The 39 Steps* (UK tour); *Love from a Stranger* (Sonning); *Betrayal* (Sir Peter Hall Co.); *Three Sisters* (Birmingham Rep and UK tour); *Presence* (Theatre Royal Plymouth); *Question Time* (Arcola); *The Changing Room* (Duke of York's); *Holidays* (West Yorkshire Playhouse); *Return of the Native* (Worcester); *A Midsummer Night's Dream, The Winter's Tale, Babes in Arms* (Regent's Park); *A Taste of Honey* and *An Enemy of the People* (Nottingham Playhouse); *A View from the Bridge* (Aldwych); *Mumbo Jumbo* (Royal Exchange, Manchester); *God Say Amen* (English Shakespeare Co.) and *Fuente Ovejuna* (National Theatre). Television credits include: *Hidden, New Tricks, Donovan, William and Mary, If...Things Don't Get Better, As Time Goes By, Family Affairs, Heartbeat, Coronation Street, Missing, Spooks, Peak Practice, Where the Heart Is, Bambino Mio, Poirot, Money for Nothing, Tube Stories, Body Stories – Crash* and *Inspector Morse*. Film credits includes: *Welcome to the Punch, Jump, Nowhere in Africa* (Oscar winner Best Foreign Language Film 2003).

creative team

Lucinda Coxon | Playwright

Lucinda Coxon's plays include: *Waiting at the Water's Edge* and *Wishbones* (Bush); *Three Graces* (Lakeside); *The Ice Palace* and a translation of Lorca's *The Shoemaker's Incredible Wife* (National Theatre Connections); *Nostalgia* and *Vesuvius* (South Coast Repertory Theater); *The Eternal Not* and the award-winning *Happy Now?* (National Theatre). Her screenplays include *The Heart of Me*, *Wild Target* and *The Crimson Petal and The White*.

Anthony Banks | Director

Anthony Banks is Associate Director for the National Theatre Discover Programme. Recent directing includes: Bryony Lavery's *More Light*, Lucinda Coxon's *The Eternal Not* and Michael Lesslie's *Prince of Denmark* (National Theatre); Calderón's *El Gran Teatro Del Mundo* (Royal Festival Hall); Snoo Wilson's *Pignight* (Menier Chocolate Factory); Doug Lucie's *Shellshock* (BBC); Mark Ravenhill's *The Experiment* (Soho, Berliner Ensemble and New York) and James Graham's *Bassett* (Bristol Old Vic). In 2012 he is directing a nationwide tour of Dennis Kelly's *DNA* and a new play by Bryony Lavery.

Garance Marneur | Designer

Garance Marneur studied fine art in Paris before graduating in Design for Performance from Central St Martins in London. She designs set and costume for theatre, dance and opera, with credits including: *The Chairs* and *Gagarin Way* (Theatre Royal Bath); the national tour of *Huck*, *Romeo and Juliet* (Stadttheater Bern, Switzerland); the multi-award-winning *Orphans* (Traverse, Edinburgh, Birmingham Rep and Soho); *Turandot* (Hampstead – winning design of the Linbury Prize for Stage Design); *Gianni Schicchi* conducted by Valery Gergiev (Mariinsky Theatre, St Petersburg); *dirty butterfly* (Young Vic); and *I Am Falling* (Gate and Sadler's Wells – nominated for a South Bank Show Award). Garance Marneur was the 2007 overall winner of the Linbury Biennial Prize for Stage Design held at the National Theatre in London.

James Mackenzie | Lighting Designer

James Mackenzie trained in lighting design at Rose Bruford College. Recent credits include: *The Gingerbread House* (Feral Productions); *In the Dust, Still Breathing* (2Faced Dance Company); *Steam* (Royal Festival Hall); *Cut It Out* (Young Vic); *Macbeth* (Courtyard, Hereford); *See* (Company Declarge); *Headcase* (Full Force Dance Company) and *Speaking in Tongues* (Birmingham School of Acting). In addition to this, James is the Director of ZOO Venues, the award-winning Edinburgh Festival Fringe venue.

Alex Baranowski | Composer and Sound Designer

Alex Baranowski is a graduate of Paul McCartney's LIPA. Theatre credits include: *Earthquakes in London*, *Hamlet* and *Frankenstein* at the National Theatre (the latter working with electro duo Underworld), with both *Hamlet* and *Frankenstein* broadcast live to cinemas as part of 'NT Live'. Other recent theatre credits include: *Salt, Root and Roe* (Donmar, Trafalgar); *The Faith Machine* (Royal Court); *Othello*, *Hobson's Choice* (Sheffield Crucible); *Mixed Marriage* (Finborough); *The Merchant of Venice* (with Adam Cork, RSC); *Bassett* (Bristol Old Vic); *Rose* (Pleasance). Dance includes: work with *Ballet Black* at the Royal Opera House Covent Garden and *In the Dust* for 2Faced Dance Company European tour. Television and film credits include: *Made in England*, *NFA*, *I Won't Go*, *Schools of Thought* and *TreQuarti*. www.alexbaranowski.co.uk

Mark Cartwright | Associate Producer

Mark Cartwright has recently produced: *Bunny* (Soho and 59E59 Theaters, New York); *Blue Surge* (Finborough) and *The Boy on the Swing* (Arcola). Other producing credits include: *Time Warner Ignite 1* and *The 24 Hour Plays: Old Vic New Voices* (Old Vic), and he was Assistant Producer on Caryl Churchill's *Light Shining in Buckinghamshire* (Arcola). He produced *One from the Heart*, a Tom Waits concept show featuring a thirteen-piece jazz orchestra at the Edinburgh Festival Fringe, and as a student produced the OUDS/Thelma Holt 2009 tour of *Henry V* (Trafalgar Studios 2 and Rustaveli Theatre in Tbilisi), as well as *A Few Good Men* at the Oxford Playhouse. In 2012 he will produce Eugene O'Neill's *The Hairy Ape* at the Southwark Playhouse.

David Luff | Producer

David Luff works in both the commercial and subsidised sectors and produces a diverse mix of contemporary and classic work. His past productions include: *The Maddening Rain* (Soho, Old Red Lion, 59E59 in New York and UK tour); *Epic* (Soho and UK tour); *No Idea* (Young Vic, UK tour and Middle East tour to Syria and Egypt); *The Spanish Tragedy*, *Thyestes*, *The Four Seasons*, *The Voyage of the Demeter* and *Tartuffe* (Arcola); *Orwell – A Celebration* (Trafalgar Studios); *Stoopud Fucken Animals* (Traverse, Edinburgh); *Dogfight* (Underbelly, Edinburgh); *Oh, My Green Soap Box* (Pleasance, Edinburgh); *Forgotten Peacock* (Brunswick Gallery), and two festivals of new performance entitled *Shortcuts* (Arcola in 2005 and Union in 2006). He is a recipient of the Stage One Producers' Bursary and previously curated the LAB Project in Berlin.

DAVID LUFF
PRODUCTIONS

herding cats

Playwright Lucinda Coxon and director Anthony Banks discuss the play.

Anthony Banks   Lucinda and I have worked together before. A couple of years ago when we began working on *The Eternal Not*, a new play I'd asked her to write for the National Theatre inspired by Shakespeare's *All's Well That Ends Well*, she asked if she could send me a play she had just finished so that I could see the type of work she was currently interested in writing. The play she sent was *Herding Cats*. She'd written it for herself, not as a commission, not to order.

Lucinda Coxon   I partly needed to write it because I'd been working a lot in film. By day I was writing the screenplay for a mainstream romantic comedy, which seemed to be in its ninety-fifth draft, and I was stuck down the joke-mine with my hammer, chiselling away. By night, I started to write this new play as an antidote to that saccharine screenplay.

When I finished the play, I sent it, rather nervously – because it wasn't what I was supposed to be working on at all – to my agent. She read it and she left me a message saying she'd call the next morning. I thought she was either furious that I'd been wasting my time or that the play was so strange she was arranging for me to be sectioned... But when she called the next morning she was terrifically supportive and we set about finding the best place for a production.

AB   Lucinda and I have been discussing the play for a long time. We've talked about its tone, its humour and how it relates to us and our lives: both of us are northerners living in the big city in the south. *Herding Cats* is a kind of conjuring trick which takes you to places you didn't know you were brave enough to venture. It explores the mess of the human condition, in a way which is at once dense, succinct, short, light on its feet and incredibly dark. I relish the way the idiom rings so recognisably in your ears – we know these people and their predicaments. It's a front-footed boulevard comedy which exists in a timeless, abstract stratosphere. Hopefully, the production will conjure the whole world of the play and the gases which fuel the three characters and their stories.

LC *Herding Cats* is a voyeuristic play in many ways. You need the audience to feel they're complicit in the action. Everything that happens is 'in camera'. The audience is spying on the action, listening in to the telephone conversations. It gives a distance and an intimacy at the same time.

It also means that we play with scale and point of view. You are inside and outside the plot, such as it is. It's a hymn to subjectivity, so each character needs to know their own version of events. But of course, the audience brings its own subjectivity to the table too. The play is packed with stories. Some very bad things happen in them, really awful things, enough to break you. And yet it also has a fast, shiny surface, a vaudevillian aspect.

AB It's hard to say what *Herding Cats* is about in a word or a sentence without being reductive. You could say it is a play about neediness, loneliness or aloneness, though of course it's about all three. Poets, philosophers and psychoanalysts have been tussling with existentialism for decades. The bottom line is everyone is going to die alone. It's pretty much the only guarantee. The characters in *Herding Cats* mewl, whine and whimper in their way through their various lots, but no one actually ever says what it is that they would rather have, what it is that they really want!

You could say it is a comedy about loneliness... It's certainly a tragicomic play about love, albeit on an acute tilt. It's a spectacular enigma. I think some people will recognise it as a coming-of-age story, approaching the milestone of reaching the age of thirty having worked diligently to become a proper adult, only to be struck by the biggest and most startling question of all: 'What's the fucking point?!!!'

LC The most shocking thing in the play, I think, is the moment when Justine says: 'I'm going to fall in love.' It's astonishing! The play describes a universe in which that is the most terrifying, reckless, revealing thing that any of the characters could possibly come up with. What does it suggest, after all? Some sincere belief in a possible union of souls? Staggering vulnerability? Everyone is flirting with a version of wanting to fall in love in the play, but only a version of love that they can control.

AB The audience become complicit; they're the fourth character. This sequence of 'reveals' is tantalising. By the end, although everything on the microscope slide is in sharp focus, you can't work out how it shares the same Petri dish. It's the conundrum of the big city. Just as you think you've fathomed the Venn diagram of how all the characters interlock, the borders shift, and you find yourself accommodating another set of possibilities.

The design for the production suggests both a contained domestic environment which any of our characters might live in, and the Garden of Eden gone to the bad.

Justine and Michael have reached the same crisis point, but they've responded with almost opposite tactics. They're two cats in a basket: she scratches and scratches; he is all stillness, waiting for the right moment to pounce. They represent distance and intimacy, and how the two relate.

LC I've written in the use of quite aggressive sound between the scenes in the play. I didn't want the audience to have any periods of respite. I don't believe the characters in the play have any, so why should the house? I also wanted to give a sense of what's outside the room, of what each character is in flight from: because the cold womb of a room is, in its dangerous way, a sanctuary.

HERDING CATS

Lucinda Coxon

For Drakey

Characters

JUSTINE, *late twenties*

MICHAEL, *late twenties*

SADDO, *fifties, Scottish accent*

Setting

The city, the present.

This text went to press before the end of rehearsals and so may differ slightly from the play as performed.

1.

Lights up. JUSTINE, *standing, starts speaking straight away, fuming. On stage, a sofa and one of those pleather cube-stool things.* MICHAEL *on the sofa. His eyes hardly ever leave her, though there's no sexual charge to speak of between the two of them.*

JUSTINE. I *literally* exploded.

MICHAEL. Really?

JUSTINE. *Literally.* Un-fucking-believable. Un-fucking-believable.

MICHAEL. Yeah?

JUSTINE. Dealing with him… It's like… it's like…

MICHAEL. What…? Go on…

JUSTINE. Herding cats. Herding fucking cats. He's a hippy. Ex-hippy. Old hippy. Too many drugs, you know. Mind the fucking gap!

MICHAEL. Ha!

JUSTINE. Yeah. Mind the fucking gap. God.

MICHAEL. Have a drink.

JUSTINE. No, I'm too… *Look* at me…

MICHAEL. It'll help –

JUSTINE. No, it won't, not when I'm like this. Like *this* it makes it worse. Like this it's like petrol – *whoosh*!

MICHAEL. God, you poor thing. *I'm* going to…

JUSTINE. You should. Yeah. Have one for me.

MICHAEL. I will.

> MICHAEL *goes to get a drink.* JUSTINE *paces, brimming with energy.*

JUSTINE. Fucking hell. Have a big one.

MICHAEL. I will do.

JUSTINE. A really bloody huge… an Oblivion and Tonic.

MICHAEL. Yeah, a beer.

JUSTINE. Yeah whatever. Fuck.

MICHAEL. Sit down. Sit down.

JUSTINE. I will, I'm just… you know…

MICHAEL. Sure. Are you sure about the…?

JUSTINE. Drink? Yes. Shit fuck Jesus. Yes.

> I'm slowing down.

MICHAEL. Yeah?

JUSTINE. With the drinking.

> MICHAEL *agrees.*

MICHAEL. Well, maybe you should.

JUSTINE. Don't say that. Don't say that…

MICHAEL. For your health, I mean. It's not good for you.

JUSTINE. Fuck off!

MICHAEL. For *anyone.*

JUSTINE. Well, I know *that.* I mean, come on! I just can't stand it when people say: 'It's not good for you. Look at the times you feel *awful* all day.' I say: 'Yes, I do *often* feel awful all day, yes.' But it's not like it's a choice between feeling awful all day or feeling generally fucking fabulous and I'm just too stupid to see the difference…

MICHAEL. No…

JUSTINE. No, it's actually a choice between feeling awful all day or feeling awful all night. That's the choice. If I don't have a drink I feel *awful* all night…

MICHAEL. I know.

JUSTINE. And at least in the day you've got distractions.

MICHAEL. That's true…

JUSTINE. At least in the day you've got things you've got to do, to get through, to pit your fucking self against. You've got reasons to keep going. What have you got at night? *CSI* fucking *Miami*.

MICHAEL. Ha.

JUSTINE. Seriously. At least in the day there's a front to maintain. There's a… there's a person you've got to be, you know…

MICHAEL. Yeah. Yeah, I guess.

JUSTINE. You have to… you know…?

MICHAEL. Yeah…

JUSTINE. The whole time.

MICHAEL. I know, yeah.

JUSTINE. Fuck. Jesus.

I don't know.

Like herding fucking cats.

MICHAEL. You said that. That was funny.

JUSTINE *breathes a second, then the agitation rises up again.*

JUSTINE. What am I going to do with him?

MICHAEL. I don't know.

JUSTINE. He needs his backside kicking from here to kingdom come.

MICHAEL. Well, if anyone can…

JUSTINE. That's what everyone at work says. But this one… I don't know.

An extraordinary, unthinkable prospect:

I think I might have met my match. I think I finally might have –

MICHAEL. You'll be fine.

JUSTINE. He needs his backside kicking from here to kingdom come. And he knows it. That's the worse thing. He's got this thick hide of fucking smugness. You know, the –

(*She 'does' Nigel.*) 'Yes, I am a lazy bastard, I'm from the lazy-bastard generation' thing… 'And even though our pubes are grey, we still smoke loads of dope, thank you. It's organic, actually. We grow our own. We've pots of it in the conservatories of our absolutely lovely houses. Houses which are worth a fortune and totally recession-proof cos we took the precaution of buying them for sixpence before you were born. Then we just hung out in them for years on end, talking crap and blowing smoke rings and every day we were just worth more – as if by fucking magic.'

MICHAEL. I bet he's got a big house.

JUSTINE. He knows Richard Branson.

MICHAEL. Really?

JUSTINE. He says so. I couldn't bring him round here.

MICHAEL. No.

JUSTINE. He'd think we were…

MICHAEL. What?

JUSTINE. Subhuman.

MICHAEL. Subhuman. Nice.

JUSTINE. That's what he'd think. I hate him.

MICHAEL. I've not taken to him. Don't ask him over.

JUSTINE. What a total prick. Total. I should get into your game.

MICHAEL. Really?

JUSTINE. That's all I do anyway these days, pander to fucking stupid weird men who can't get it up on their own, even if it's metaphorically speaking. Your way at least there's some dignity to it. It's out in the fucking open. I should do what you do.

MICHAEL. D'you want to?

JUSTINE. I could do.

MICHAEL. Well, of course you could if...

JUSTINE. I could probably do it. I probably ought to. You could train me.

MICHAEL. If you mean it, I could always talk to the agency...

JUSTINE. God – are you serious?

MICHAEL. Well, you just said...

JUSTINE. God, no! I mean, thanks, but... Oh, I couldn't do it. Not really. You know me. I couldn't do what you do.

MICHAEL. Why not?

JUSTINE. I just couldn't. Fuck, I know my own limitations. That's over the line for me.

MICHAEL. What, morally?

JUSTINE. No, no, not *that* – you know that. More... I'd just get too cross with them.

MICHAEL. Right.

JUSTINE. You don't get cross with them.

MICHAEL. No. Not unless they ask me to.

JUSTINE. You're not even tempted. Even the really annoying ones.

MICHAEL. No. Never.

JUSTINE. I would. See, I'm cross now, just thinking about them – it's not even my job. I'm cross on your behalf.

MICHAEL. Don't be.

JUSTINE. No?

MICHAEL. No need.

JUSTINE. You think?

MICHAEL. No need. I'm fine.

JUSTINE. *Are* you? Doesn't it ever…?

MICHAEL. What?

JUSTINE. Affect you. You never seem… I mean, look at me, but you…

MICHAEL. I don't think so.

JUSTINE. Having to…

MICHAEL. It's only pretend.

JUSTINE. Still. It's intense.

MICHAEL. Sometimes.

JUSTINE. How do you keep it from… I wouldn't be able to…

MICHAEL. What?

JUSTINE. Keep a distance. Maintain a healthy distance.

MICHAEL. Well, then you shouldn't do it.

JUSTINE. No. In any case, I've got a job. I've got a job. I've got the job I always wanted.

MICHAEL. Exactly.

JUSTINE. A job other people would kill for. Especially *these* days. The state everything's in.

MICHAEL. They'd give their eye teeth.

JUSTINE. People do it for free, you know. To get a frigging look-in. Mind you, they don't last.

MICHAEL. No?

JUSTINE. The trust-fund brigade. They've not got the peasant stamina.

MICHAEL. The staying power.

JUSTINE. The appetite for shovelling shit. I'm serious. They think it'll be glamorous. They can't believe the things you have to put yourself through. The pressure, and the… well, just the *front* it takes.

MICHAEL. I know.

JUSTINE. The people you're dealing with – difficult people.

MICHAEL. I couldn't do it. I mean, back when I did it, I couldn't. Not really.

JUSTINE. Anyone could do it for a week or a month, but to keep going…

MICHAEL. Exactly.

JUSTINE. *That* is what sorts out the sheep from the goats, you know. Just… keeping going. (*A fresh crest of anger.*) God, I want a drink now. And whose fault is that?

MICHAEL. It's his fault.

JUSTINE. I'm not going to have one, though.

MICHAEL. Good for you.

JUSTINE. *Fuck* him.

MICHAEL. That's the spirit.

JUSTINE. I knew he'd be like this. I saw it coming.

MICHAEL. I remember, you said.

JUSTINE. Right from the start. 'Show him the ropes, will you?' 'Is that my job?' I said. 'Project coordinator?' 'Show

him the ropes.' I should've said *then* – 'Yes, okay, Nigel,
repeat after me: arse… elbow… arse…'

MICHAEL *sniggers.*

God, I'm already taking the piss out of him. One week in
and I'm taking the piss. What's it going to be like by
Christmas?

MICHAEL. Well, not pretty.

JUSTINE. What's worse is he doesn't even notice I'm doing it.
Even when I'm really… right in there, you know…

MICHAEL. No?

JUSTINE. It's like he's got no self-awareness at all.

MICHAEL. Really?

JUSTINE. Nothing. There's nothing you can say to him. It all
just rolls off. He doesn't care. It's like firing peas at an
elephant. That's what I'm doing. Firing peas at an elephant.
It's unbelievably annoying. I'm at my wits' fucking end
before we've even got started. I've got a pea-shooter and
what I need is a crossbow.

She fires.

Thock!

MICHAEL. That wouldn't be enough.

JUSTINE. No?

MICHAEL. On an elephant?

JUSTINE. You're right. I need a… I don't even know what I
need. I don't even know what I fucking need. I need a rifle.
An UZI. I need to empty a whole fucking magazine of stuff
into him, just to get a moment's… It still wouldn't be
enough though.

MICHAEL. No.

JUSTINE. A truck full of explosives.

MICHAEL. Take you down with him.

JUSTINE. I don't know what I need.

MICHAEL. I do.

JUSTINE. What?

Pause for effect.

MICHAEL. A mouse.

They erupt into laughter...

Transition: laughter, music – opening bars of 'Something for the Weekend' by The Divine Comedy.

2.

SADDO *on the cube stool, in an isolated pool of light.*

He's on the telephone.

The voices in this scene are softly amplified.

SADDO. Hello?

GIRL'S VOICE ON PHONE (*Scottish accent*). Hello...?

SADDO. Do you know who it is?

GIRL'S VOICE ON PHONE. Is it you...?

SADDO. Do you know...?

GIRL'S VOICE ON PHONE. Yes.

SADDO. Did you know before you even picked up the phone...?

GIRL'S VOICE ON PHONE. Daddy?

SADDO. That's right.

GIRL'S VOICE ON PHONE. Daddy.

SADDO. How are you, sweetheart...?

GIRL'S VOICE ON PHONE. Oh, I'm alright.

Another pool of light comes up. We see it's MICHAEL *on the other phone.*

SADDO. That's my girl.

A shy laugh from MICHAEL.

You've been a very good girl, haven't you?

MICHAEL. I sent you something yesterday.

SADDO. I know. I've got them. I've got them right here.

SADDO has a brown envelope.

MICHAEL. That's very fast. They reached you very quickly.

SADDO. Well, you sent them first class, sweetheart. You knew I was looking forward.

MICHAEL. Yeah.

SADDO. Didn't want me t'have to wait.

MICHAEL. No. Have you got your card there too?

SADDO. Sure.

MICHAEL. Okay then.

SADDO. It's the MasterCard.

They laugh, a shared joke.

You know the PIN.

MICHAEL*'s coy.*

MICHAEL. I shouldn't though.

SADDO. I told you it.

MICHAEL. I know you did.

SADDO. I trust you. Am I right to do that?

MICHAEL. Yes.

Yes. Course you are.

We hear four beeps as MICHAEL *enters the PIN.*

I don't take it for granted.

The moment hangs between them for a second, then:

SADDO. Your mother wouldn't like it.

MICHAEL. No.

SADDO. She'd say you'd got me round your little finger.

MICHAEL. Would she…?

SADDO. But it gives me peace of mind. Just to know, sweetheart… that if you're ever in trouble, you can always use the card. If you got stuck somewhere, I mean. You're a long way from home now.

MICHAEL. A long way.

SADDO. Your mother really misses you.

MICHAEL. I know.

SADDO. She really does.

MICHAEL. I know, Daddy.

SADDO. She says the day you left home, it was like somebody turned off the sun.

MICHAEL *sighs, then:*

MICHAEL. Your card just cleared, Daddy.

SADDO. Always does. Always will. Always kept on top of that side of things.

MICHAEL. Do you miss me, Daddy?

SADDO. Oh, you know I do, princess.

MICHAEL. Are you missing me now, Daddy…?

SADDO. Oh, I miss you all the time. I miss you hard. I miss you so I ache all over, sweetheart, and I don't know what I can do to feel better.

MICHAEL. Do you have the panties?

SADDO. I do, yes. I have them right here.

SADDO *takes out a pair of women's knickers.*

MICHAEL. Are you sniffing them, Daddy?

SADDO. I am.

MICHAEL. Is there anything I can do to help you now, Daddy?

SADDO. You know what to do. You always know just what to do.

The light fades on MICHAEL, *leaving* SADDO *isolated, the underwear over his mouth and nose. Then blackout.*

Transition: the opening bars of '9 to 5' by Dolly Parton.

3.

JUSTINE *and* MICHAEL.

JUSTINE *speaks straight away, an undercurrent of fear driving her.*

JUSTINE. He asked me to tie his toes together.

MICHAEL. He what?

JUSTINE. We were sitting going through the schedule, he put his feet up in my lap.

MICHAEL. Fuck. Cheeky.

JUSTINE. I said: 'What's this?' He said: 'I think I've got nice feet. I never used to. When I was younger, I was self-conscious about them. You're self-conscious about a lot of things when you're young, but now I think they're fine.'

MICHAEL. What did you say?

JUSTINE. I didn't say anything.

MICHAEL. Not even…

JUSTINE. I just sat there. I was stunned. I was literally stunned.

MICHAEL. And then?

JUSTINE. And then he said: 'Why don't you tie my toes together?' And he laughed.

MICHAEL. He laughed?

JUSTINE. As if it was funny. He said: 'That pretty ribbon belt…'

MICHAEL. That one.

JUSTINE. This one.

MICHAEL. You got that in the Gap.

JUSTINE. I know.

MICHAEL. It's lovely.

JUSTINE. I don't want it any more. I can't even stand the idea of it.

MICHAEL. That's silly.

JUSTINE. 'That pretty ribbon belt,' he said. 'Why don't you slip it off and tie my two big toes together?'

MICHAEL. Fuck.

JUSTINE*'s angry, but we see, increasingly, the distress and revulsion underpinning it.*

JUSTINE. So I said: 'Why would I want to do that, Nigel?' And he shrugged – like – y'know, like this big smug-fuck shrug – like this – and he said: 'I don't know. Just t'see what happens next.'

MICHAEL. And what did happen next?

JUSTINE. I didn't do it.

MICHAEL. What did you do?

JUSTINE. I just looked at him. I thought – I am really good at my job and I will not be intimidated by a prick like you. And I stared him down.

MICHAEL. You good girl. And?

JUSTINE. And eventually he took his feet off.

MICHAEL. Did he say anything?

JUSTINE. He said: 'You make me laugh.' And then he laughed. He said: 'You funny girl, you make me laugh.'

MICHAEL. Fuck. *Fuck!*

JUSTINE. And so I said: 'Nigel, actually, that wasn't very funny.'

MICHAEL. Did you?

JUSTINE. Well, not straight away. I couldn't say *anything* straight away.

MICHAEL. No…

JUSTINE. But later, after he'd gone out and come back in again… I don't know, he must've seen I was…

JUSTINE *shies away from recalling being upset.*

MICHAEL. What?

JUSTINE. I don't know… something.

MICHAEL. Upset?

JUSTINE. *Yes.* And he said: 'Oh my God, look at your face' – but he said it in this kind, surprised way, like he gave a shit. And I said: 'What?' And he puts his hands on his hips and he tilts his head and he says: 'Justine, I'm really sorry. It was a joke. I didn't mean to make you feel uncomfortable.' I said I didn't feel uncomfortable.

MICHAEL. But you did.

JUSTINE. *Of course* I did. He said: 'I didn't mean to scare you,' I said: 'You didn't scare me, Nigel. It's just that as jokes go, that wasn't especially funny.' And he said: 'Well, Justine, I apologise unreservedly. Believe me, *you're the last person in this place I'd want to upset.*'

MICHAEL. God…

JUSTINE. Well, what does that mean?

MICHAEL. I'm not sure… I think it's good, though, don't you?

JUSTINE. He said: '*Really.* I don't know what I'd do without you.' I fucking snapped right back at him – I said: 'Let's hope you never have to find out!'

MICHAEL. You didn't…

JUSTINE. I did. I did, and I think he heard that. Because it's *true* – they would be up shit creek without me. They'd be up shit creek without a paddle. They're totally dependent. Totally.

So he spent all afternoon shut up in his office, and I thought just for once he might be doing something useful – you can see what a fool I am! I thought after what happened he might pull his finger out.

So eventually, he comes out and says he's got something he wants me to look through.

MICHAEL. Yes…?

JUSTINE. It turns out, he's only cut up the schedule and rearranged it – I mean, he's actually cut it up with scissors and Pritt-Sticked it all back together and re-photocopied it and then put like arrows all over it and there's his stupid fucking handwriting and then there's another arrow and a fucking asterisk and… I mean, I'm reeling. It's just unbelievable. It's going to take – I promise you – *for ever* to unravel. Literally. For ever. The knock-on effect is just staggering. Plus, I can't analyse it like that, so it's all got to be input again before I can even see how much damage he's actually done. It just beggars belief.

I said: 'Couldn't you at least have done it on the computer?' He said: 'I'm not good with technology.' I said: 'You can manage your fucking iPad alright though, can't you?'

MICHAEL. You didn't.

JUSTINE. I did, I said: 'Well, you manage alright with your iPad, I notice.' And he just smiles, you know. He just smiles. Then: 'Someone gave it me, the iPad,' he says. 'Oh, Richard Branson?' I go. And he laughs and says: 'No, no, some rep.' Happens all the time, apparently, you know, that he gets given things. I said: 'That's nice getting given things like that.'

MICHAEL. Yeah. *Big* things.

JUSTINE. 'Happens all the time,' he says. 'This leather jacket, for example, I didn't pay for it.' And I'm so minded to say: 'Well, *good*, because that would make you an accomplice, sir. That blouson atrocity is wanted for crimes against fashion from Land's End to John O'Fucking Groats!'

MICHAEL. You fucking should have.

JUSTINE. I came so fucking close.

MICHAEL. You should. You should say it tomorrow!

JUSTINE *sinks a little, not encouraged. She shakes her head, despairing.*

JUSTINE. *Shit.* I mean, I work hard, Michael.

MICHAEL. I know you do.

JUSTINE. What time was I in there this morning?

MICHAEL. Oh – early.

JUSTINE. It was early.

MICHAEL. It was still dark when you…

JUSTINE. Dark when I leave in the fucking… still dark when I get home. In between: herding cats. And there still isn't time for anything. It's still fucking mental all day. And then I get back here and I haven't got time to do even the laundry. I haven't even got any clean fucking clothes. I've run out of knickers completely – it's like they just vanish.

MICHAEL. I know, I know.

JUSTINE. And he just smells like bloody fabric softener all the time. Because someone else does all that for him. He doesn't do anything. He doesn't do anything while he's at home and then he comes into work and he doesn't do anything all over again. And when he does do something it's a disaster! I said to Chris Markham: 'He's not even any good.' And you know what Chris said? He said, he said: 'He's good enough. For what we're doing, he's good enough.'

Fucking hell! What are we living in? I hate that. Good enough. I sometimes feel like I'm the only one there who still takes… takes *pride* in… who actually… you know, inside, still…

Shit…

I don't know.

I'm good at what I do, you know.

MICHAEL. I know you are.

JUSTINE. I'm really fucking good at it. I'm better, actually, than I need to be.

MICHAEL. That's probably the case.

JUSTINE. I go the extra fucking mile. I take the high road.

MICHAEL. I know you do. I know.

JUSTINE. I can't stand letting people down. You know that.

MICHAEL *nods.*

Now this.

He's a truly lazy fucker. I cover for him all the time.

And now he just did this to me.

MICHAEL. Just let it go.

JUSTINE. He really is a fucking pig.

MICHAEL. He is a total fucking pig.

JUSTINE. And now I need a fucking drink. And we all know whose fault that is.

Transition: opening bars of 'This Charming Man' by The Smiths.

4.

SADDO, *on the phone.*

SADDO. Do you remember when you couldn't get to sleep at night? I'd sing to you. Do you remember the things I used to sing?

He sings the opening few lines of 'What Kind of Fool Am I?'

Lights reveal MICHAEL, also on the phone, apparently lost in the world of the song.

You used to love that song.

MICHAEL. I still do.

SADDO. Do you?

MICHAEL. *Love* it.

SADDO. Do you think of it in bed at night?

MICHAEL. Often, I think of it. Any time I can't get to sleep, I sing it over in my head.

SADDO. Oh, that's a lovely thing for me to know.

MICHAEL. It's true, though.

SADDO. You sing it to yourself and think of me.

MICHAEL. I think of you and I feel very safe then.

SADDO. And it helps you. To relax.

MICHAEL. It really does.

SADDO. And what else do you do, to relax, princess…?

MICHAEL. I'm not sure I know what you mean, Daddy?

SADDO. While you sing it to yourself, what else do you do…?

MICHAEL. While I'm singing it?

SADDO. Mm-hm.

MICHAEL *hesitates a moment, then:*

MICHAEL. I think nice thoughts.

SADDO. About what?

MICHAEL. All sorts. You know. Happy things.

SADDO. Do you think about me sometimes?

MICHAEL. Oh, it's always you, Daddy.

SADDO *seems genuinely moved, gratified.*

SADDO. Oh, that's nice.

MICHAEL. Yeah.

SADDO. That's nice to hear…

Beat.

And what else do you do, while you're singing to yourself and you're thinking these nice thoughts about me…

Beat.

Juliet…?

MICHAEL *sighs.*

MICHAEL. Don't be cross with me, Daddy…

SADDO. I won't be cross with you.

MICHAEL. Promise me.

SADDO. Tell me what you do, sweetheart.

MICHAEL *hesitates, then:*

MICHAEL. I don't think I can tell you.

SADDO. Oh, you've always told me everything. We don't have secrets, you and me. What's your mother always saying: you couldn't get a hair between them.

MICHAEL *laughs softly.*

MICHAEL. Yeah.

SADDO. So you tell me.

MICHAEL. Well… if you really want to know…

SADDO. I do…

MICHAEL *breathes, then:*

MICHAEL. I touch myself.

SADDO. Do you?

MICHAEL. Yes, Daddy. That song goes round in my head and
I… I touch myself…

SADDO. Down below?

MICHAEL. Yes.

SADDO. I see.

The sound of both, just breathing for a moment, then:

Do you get your fingers sticky…?

MICHAEL. Yes.

SADDO. You get yourself all puffed up and sticky…?

MICHAEL. Yes, I do.

SADDO. And then what?

MICHAEL. Do you promise you won't be cross with me,
Daddy?

SADDO. I promise.

MICHAEL. I go inside.

SADDO. You touch yourself inside?

MICHAEL. I do.

A moment of silence, then SADDO*'s voice, low, altered…*

SADDO. Oh, Juliet…

MICHAEL. Are you angry, Daddy?

SADDO. No. Not angry.

   Not that, no. But I am…

MICHAEL. What…?

SADDO. Well, I'm disappointed.

   MICHAEL*'s tone shifts, anxiety creeping in.*

MICHAEL. I'm so sorry. Am I in trouble now?

SADDO. I'm afraid so.

   There's fear now.

MICHAEL. I'm sorry…

SADDO. This is for your own good.

MICHAEL. Yes. I understand that.

   SADDO *shakes his head. Genuine despair.*

SADDO. Oh, Juliet…

MICHAEL. Are you taking off your belt now, Daddy…?

   SADDO *reconciles himself to the horrible truth.*

SADDO. You've not really left me a great deal of choice.

   Lights fade on MICHAEL *as* SADDO *unbuckles his belt, runs the leather through his hands, sickened at the thought of what's to come. Lights out. Music in transition: 'I Touch Myself' by The Divinyls.*

5.

JUSTINE *and* MICHAEL.

JUSTINE *has tinsel in her hair. She's just come in, still on a high.* MICHAEL *pours drinks for both of them – not the first of the night.*

JUSTINE. So he looks at me – like this – and he says: 'I don't know, Justine, you don't like men much, do you?'

MICHAEL. No!

JUSTINE. But I was ready for him! Do you know what I said? Do you know what I said? I said:

'I think men should be Obscene But Not Heard'!

MICHAEL. Oh my God!!! Obscene but not heard! God, that's funny!

JUSTINE. I know! I know! I couldn't believe it. It just came out because I was so cross with him. You know how sometimes when you're really really *aaagh*... when you're right in the fucking heat of it...

MICHAEL. Yeah yeah.

JUSTINE. He'd been a bastard all day, so the minute he started in on me – I thought, oh no, Mister Sister. You have *so* picked the wrong one tonight. It just... *zing*! Hah. I said it. Plus – Christmas party – who cares, right?

MICHAEL. So what did he say?

JUSTINE. He tried not to smile. He tried not to smile but he couldn't... I could see his mouth all sort of twitching round the edges – he's got a nice mouth actually – and then he said, very cool, you know: 'That's very good. You ought to work in comedy.'

MICHAEL. Oh – shit – that could go either way.

JUSTINE. I know, and for a moment I thought he'd bloody got me, but then… his face cracked open.

MICHAEL. Yeah?!

JUSTINE. He couldn't keep it going, see? And he smiled this ridiculous smile – and it was a cover smile, I could see that, cos he bloody knew he was on the ropes – and he said: 'You know what, Justine: you are the Devil.'

MICHAEL gasps, excited.

MICHAEL. You've so got him!

JUSTINE. And I was on such a roll… I only said: 'The Devil? Well, you're close, but no cigar there, Nige… cos actually…'

She's so excited, she can hardly finish.

'…I'm the *Pantychrist*.' And I just walked off!

JUSTINE and MICHAEL are beside themselves.

MICHAEL. The Pantychrist!

JUSTINE. Can you believe it!

MICHAEL. That just came out!?

JUSTINE. I shouldn't drink absinthe.

MICHAEL. That's the funniest thing I've ever heard!

JUSTINE. It's him. He inspires me.

She pours more drinks.

MICHAEL. I'm starting to like him.

JUSTINE. *Don't.* Don't don't don't don't, no. We mustn't. Cos he's actually a total shit.

MICHAEL. I know, but still…

JUSTINE. But still. It is funny.

MICHAEL. You've got him on the run now.

JUSTINE. I think I have!

MICHAEL. He's not going to give you any more trouble.

JUSTINE. I think that's right. I think that's right. God.

They clink glasses.

MICHAEL. I knew you'd do it. Turn the tables.

JUSTINE. Well, *I* didn't – it's a big relief. Cos I was scared, you know. I didn't say but I was actually scared.

MICHAEL. Why scared? That's ridiculous!

JUSTINE. I know. I don't know. But it's alright now.

MICHAEL. Yeah. Now he knows where he stands!

JUSTINE. I went over to talk to Mary Kane and all that lot and Mary said to me, she said: 'We feel sorry for you. We don't know how you stand it. You're the only one who can manage him.' And I said: 'He's just a child. You got to treat him like a child.' She said: 'I don't think he's a child, I think he's selfish, dark, and fucked-up.'

MICHAEL *registers this with some anxiety.*

MICHAEL. Really?

JUSTINE. But she just doesn't get him. I mean, I like Mary but she's straight up and down. I said he's not as bad as all that. You get used to him.

MICHAEL. God, they're lucky to have you!

JUSTINE. I think that's right, actually. She said Liz in accounts had one like him once, made life a misery. She used t'rinse out his mug in the loo.

MICHAEL. That's not nice.

JUSTINE. That's what I said. Was all that kept her going, Mary said. Watching him drinking his green tea out of it.

MICHAEL. Nigel better watch out!

JUSTINE. Yeah, but you know what, after I walked off and talked to the others, he just stayed put where he was. I thought he'd be off and working the room and that. Or going to something glitzier – did I tell you he knows that one from REM?

MICHAEL. Not –

JUSTINE. Not him, no, one of the other ones. Anyway. He stayed put. And every now and then, he looked over at me, you know. And I thought – God, he's about as much use as a chocolate teapot, but once you get the hang of him…

MICHAEL. You've worked at it.

JUSTINE. And once he knows he *needs* you.

MICHAEL. Well, exactly.

JUSTINE. So I gave it a minute and went back and talked to him.

MICHAEL. Well, that's nice.

JUSTINE. Well, I'd got a bit of an agenda, actually.

MICHAEL. Oh – say more…

JUSTINE. I said: 'I'm surprised you're still here, Nigel, surprised you've not got bigger fish to fry.' He said: 'D'you know, I'm much less interesting than you seem to think,' and I nearly said: 'You couldn't be!' But there was something about him and I didn't… He said: 'I'm gunna hang on here a bit longer then head home.' And he said 'home' in this funny way, you know, like he wasn't in any hurry t'get there… He seemed a bit down to be honest. I don't think the marriage is up to much.

MICHAEL. Well, I'm not surprised with what he's like.

JUSTINE. He can be nice.

MICHAEL. He's not very often, though.

JUSTINE. Except he's not *not* nice, he's just… difficult. He's odd. I felt sorry for him.

MICHAEL. Why?!

JUSTINE. He was drinking the melted ice from the bottom of his glass – he can't drink much, see, cos he's got to drive home.

MICHAEL (*correcting the picture*). To the country pile!

JUSTINE. Well, I know, but… just listen… Listen, he said: 'So who do you go home to at the end of the day, Justine? It's funny how I've never asked. Perhaps I don't really want to know.'

MICHAEL. Get off – where's he going with that?

JUSTINE. Oh, I don't know, but the timing was perfect cos I wanted to talk to him about *you*, y'see. That was my agenda.

MICHAEL*'s surprised.*

MICHAEL. Why?

JUSTINE. Well, why not…?

(*Confesses.*) Y'know, in a month we'll be snowed under, Michael. I don't mean you'd like come into the office, but there's always stuff could be done from home. You'd be perfect for it. You'd be a lifesaver…

MICHAEL. So what did you tell him about me?

JUSTINE. I told him how I'd met you when me and Chris Markham were on that Irish job –

MICHAEL. God – that was chaos!

JUSTINE. Chaos didn't cover that one! Anyway, I said you came in to do temping and you were just like the *biggest* help. I said you were brilliant on the phone.

MICHAEL *rolls his eyes.*

No, but *really*. Cos you are.

He takes the compliment.

I didn't mention the ME.

Something in MICHAEL *recoils.*

MICHAEL. It might not be ME.

JUSTINE. No, I know. Besides, I thought it might make you sound… you know, unreliable. Which you're not. I said you couldn't go out, agoraphobia – I didn't know what else to…

MICHAEL. That's alright. I don't mind. That might even be right.

JUSTINE. I said something had happened…. you'd had an accident, you know, been attacked…

MICHAEL. Did you say 'attacked'?

JUSTINE. 'Mugged' maybe, I might have said. But I didn't go into the details.

MICHAEL (*firmly*). You don't know the details.

JUSTINE. Exactly. I know. But I said it had left you… well… in shock, I suppose. I thought that was accurate without being too…

MICHAEL. No…

JUSTINE. I didn't want to say too much.

MICHAEL. Right.

JUSTINE. I wasn't trying to tell him the truth exactly, just like a version of it he could get his head round.

MICHAEL. Sure. Sure.

JUSTINE. And he was very sympathetic actually. I mean, in so far as he's capable.

MICHAEL. What did he say?

JUSTINE. Well, he didn't say anything, but he pulled a face, like a 'Jesus – poor bugger' face. And he said just last year he'd got caught in this bomb scare, and he thought he'd really had it. He said the world's a really violent place now.

MICHAEL. I see.

JUSTINE. He said he thought his generation was really lucky growing up, cos they didn't have to deal with all the things we have to deal with. I said I never think about it. I don't think people my age do. You couldn't, could you, not and keep going? Besides, there isn't *time*.

MICHAEL. No…

JUSTINE. So anyway, he said if I trust you, he trusts you. So I said: 'Well, I trust him *absolutely*,' so that's done.

MICHAEL. Just like that?

JUSTINE. The thing is, he trusts *me*. So it's there if you want it.

MICHAEL. Thank you. It's really kind.

JUSTINE. I thought it might do you good.

MICHAEL. Maybe. Though I am busy. Things are hotting up.

JUSTINE. But to do something different. Back in the mainstream. A bit less…

MICHAEL. Oh, don't come that! You just had your office Christmas party in a strip club!

JUSTINE. Burlesque. And it wasn't my idea – you know I was really pissed off about that.

MICHAEL *smiles – he knows.*

MICHAEL. I know you were – and I will think, I promise you…

JUSTINE *accepts this. A moment's peace, then:*

JUSTINE. I worry about you.

MICHAEL. Why?

JUSTINE. I'm worried about you being all on your own over Christmas. It's not a time to be on your own.

MICHAEL. No, it's a time to be miserable with family.

JUSTINE. You'd be welcome at ours. It would be nice for me. Like a human shield.

MICHAEL. You do make it sound tempting.

JUSTINE. It would be funny, I promise you.

She gets up, pours more drinks.

It's the same every year – I get home and they've not even got the tree up yet cos I'm the only one who can get up the loft ladder. She gets vertigo and he's too fat to fit through the fucking hatch.

They laugh.

Then we'll have the whole thing where my dad goes through the dead fairy lights looking for the dodgy bulb – hello people! – newsflash – buy some new lights, they're like eight ninety-nine, you know! Then Christmas Day, in the paper hats… God… And afterwards, the fucking… y'know… *silence.*

She grimaces at the horror. Then:

I honestly think you'd think it was funny…

MICHAEL. It sounds awful.

JUSTINE. It's not, it's just… normal.

MICHAEL. I'll be fine. And I'll be working, mostly.

JUSTINE. On Christmas Day?

MICHAEL. Apparently it gets very busy in the afternoon.

JUSTINE. I'm not surprised actually. I hate it after lunch.

MICHAEL. Well, there's nothing to look forward to by then, is there?

JUSTINE. That's when you drink the stupid drinks.

MICHAEL. Anyway, lots of the other girls have got kids, so they don't *want* to work Christmas, so I'm thinking I might do quite well out of it.

JUSTINE *starts to laugh.*

JUSTINE. 'Other girls' – you've started believing your own publicity.

MICHAEL. The real girls, I mean. You know that.

JUSTINE *lies down, the drink and tiredness kicking in.*

JUSTINE. So was it busy today?

MICHAEL. Oh, it was good, thanks – a few regulars and then a couple of new ones. Got them through the chatroom, which I was pleased about. I think that's going to be a winner. It was maybe a little bit slower than usual, but… I figure this time of year…

JUSTINE. Everyone's last-minute shopping. Who were the regulars?

MICHAEL. Oh, your favourite called.

JUSTINE. The one with the special machine…?

MICHAEL *nods.*

Did he make you bigger or smaller today?

MICHAEL. He made me tiny.

JUSTINE. How tiny?

MICHAEL. Like an ant. And I had to wiggle up inside his cock, and then he spewed me out, surfing a great tide of jizz, like SeaWorld gone to the bad.

They laugh.

JUSTINE. He's hilarious.

MICHAEL. He's okay.

JUSTINE. Who else?

MICHAEL. The Scat Cat. I've got to work on my sound
    effects. I think he rumbled me pouring the water into the
    bucket. He said he was expecting more pressure.

JUSTINE. Oh God…

MICHAEL. I've emptied the Fairy Liquid to try out the
    squeezy bottle. Will you phone me and listen to it
    tomorrow?

JUSTINE. I'd be delighted.

MICHAEL. One of the new ones wants me do it with his wife.
    I thought that sounded fun.

JUSTINE. Nice.

MICHAEL. And I can tell he'll be orchestrating the whole
    thing, you know. He's quite… clear… quite methodical. I
    like that. I like the ones that know what they want.

JUSTINE. Who else, of the regulars?

MICHAEL. Saddo. Of course.

JUSTINE. Of course.

There's a slight shift in mood.

What did he want?

MICHAEL. The usual.

JUSTINE. Tell me.

MICHAEL. No.

JUSTINE. Yes.

MICHAEL. No.

JUSTINE. Why?

MICHAEL. Just because.

JUSTINE. Why because?

MICHAEL *takes her in.*

MICHAEL. Because you're inclined to ask questions before you've thought about whether or not you can handle the answer.

JUSTINE. Am I?

Can I not handle this?

MICHAEL. No.

JUSTINE. Why not? If you can.

MICHAEL. It's different.

JUSTINE. I tell you everything.

MICHAEL. Maybe you shouldn't.

JUSTINE. Can I not handle it?

MICHAEL. No.

JUSTINE. I'll only imagine it worse.

MICHAEL. No, Justine.

JUSTINE. I've an everso vivid imagination.

MICHAEL. Still.

JUSTINE. Right.

She takes him in, genuinely intrigued.

God. I don't know how you get to sleep at night.

MICHAEL. I sing to myself, in my head.

Transition: 'Jingle Bells' comes up, the super-perky Gene Autry version, and continues over:

6.

SADDO, JUSTINE *and* MICHAEL.

Christmas. A fantasia. The following should be considered minimum requirement:

'Jingle Bells' plays over SADDO *hurrying on, happy happy happy, with his Christmas tree. Switches on his lights – and they work!* JUSTINE *runs on to string a paper garland across the stage, full of hope, of excitement. They're in separate but unified spaces. A fantasy. A party popper explodes onto the stage, spraying tinsel streamers and sparkling confetti...* SADDO *and* JUSTINE *are caught by surprise and then* MICHAEL *comes on – the culprit! – fires another popper, laughing. The others find this charming, hilarious. A remarkable sense of harmonious collaboration... It's the best Christmas ever!*

MICHAEL *produces three crackers. They form a circle and pull... kerpow! They collect up their favours, hats, retreat, excited into their separate spaces...*

They each read their terrible jokes and as the music begins to fade slightly, isolation sets in, gloom begins to gather...

JUSTINE*'s the first to admit defeat... a slow creeping disillusion filling her... She snaps, pulls down the paper garland, disconsolate. Goes off...*

There's a growing tension between MICHAEL *and* SADDO, *in spite of their being in separate spaces... A longing... Then* SADDO *breaks away, takes the angel off the top of his tree... considers it... blanking* MICHAEL...

MICHAEL *starts tidying up all the streamers, clearing up the crap, the streamer and cracker rubbish, goes off as the lights fade, leaving* SADDO *alone with his tree as the music gathers itself to a great climactic nothing...*

7.

JUSTINE *and* MICHAEL.

JUSTINE *is about to burst.*

JUSTINE. He said he really missed me.

> MICHAEL*'s eyes open wide.*

MICHAEL. When?

JUSTINE. At Christmas.

MICHAEL. Oh, shut up…

JUSTINE. He says it caught him totally but completely by surprise.

MICHAEL. Fucking Ada. That's outrageous…

JUSTINE. I know it is. I told him that. Not in so many, but still…

MICHAEL. He's lost his… He just came out with it?

JUSTINE. No…

> *She baffles slightly…* MICHAEL *can't wait.*

MICHAEL. Justine!

JUSTINE: 'Don't let me smoke,' he says first. 'If I get the packet out, stop me. Do whatever you have to. I give you full licence. I want you to save me from myself.'

MICHAEL. Shit.

JUSTINE. It's his New Year's Resolution to smoke less – not to give up, he thought that was ambitious. He says the perfect is the enemy of the good. He says he'd rather set the bar low and achieve something small than just fail fail fail

fail. And then he asked me what my New Year's Resolutions were. I told him this year I hadn't made any. I said I'd had enough of that shit. I said I wanted things to be *really* different this time round, so I wasn't making resolutions, I was issuing *demands* instead.

MICHAEL. Oh my God! What did he say?

JUSTINE. He asked me what I was demanding!

MICHAEL. And?

JUSTINE. I couldn't think! Can you bloody believe it! I couldn't think. And then I said: 'I think this year I'm going to fall in love.'

MICHAEL. You did not!

JUSTINE. I did.

MICHAEL*'s amazed, faintly appalled.*

MICHAEL. Why?!

JUSTINE. I don't know. I just said it and then I said: 'And I think I'm going to be bloody brilliant at it!'

MICHAEL. You're a fucking nutcase!

JUSTINE. I know. You should have seen his face. He was so shocked.

MICHAEL. I'm not surprised.

JUSTINE. He was so shocked – that I just put it out there. I thought yes, you hippy fucker, chew on that. I wanted to show him.

MICHAEL. Show him what?

JUSTINE. That even if you sometimes fail it's worth aiming for something higher. I wanted to be better than him.

MICHAEL. You already are.

JUSTINE. I know I am. And *that's when he said it*. He said: 'You know, I really missed you.' And I was like: 'Oh, I missed you too, Nigel.' *Not*. And he looked a bit sorry for himself and said:

'No – *really*.'

And the whole tone sort of shifted. So I said: 'You make me laugh.' I thought… put him back in his box, but he said:

JUSTINE *'does' Nigel's low, intimate tone.*

'Why? What's so funny about that? Why is it you find that so hard to take seriously?'

MICHAEL. Fuck.

JUSTINE. I said: 'Hang on – this has come out of nowhere…' He said: 'Has it? It doesn't feel that way to me…'

So I said: 'Look, Nigel, stop this.' He said – 'Really… why?' I said: 'I just don't know where it's going.' He said: 'How about I just breathe into your neck for a while and we'll see where that takes us.'

MICHAEL. Jesus. Jesus.

JUSTINE. So he did.

MICHAEL. No!

JUSTINE. Yes.

MICHAEL. And…?

JUSTINE. And what?

MICHAEL. Well, for goodness' sake, Justine!

JUSTINE. I don't know… I just let it go on for a bit…

MICHAEL. It wasn't…?

JUSTINE. What?

MICHAEL. Nice?

JUSTINE. Oh, it was nice… it was…

MICHAEL. What…?

JUSTINE. Fucking hell, it was terrifying, but…

MICHAEL. But what…

JUSTINE. Well, I said: 'Look, can we stop this a minute?'

MICHAEL. Why?

JUSTINE. Well, we're in the fucking office, you know?

MICHAEL. So…

JUSTINE. I mean, I was…

MICHAEL. Yes, go on…

JUSTINE. I could hardly stand up. I said: 'Nigel, I'm not sure I can work like this.'

MICHAEL. And what did he say?

JUSTINE. He said: 'Justine, I think you underestimate yourself.'

MICHAEL (*undercurrent of admiration*). The cheeky sod.

JUSTINE (*still in the grip of it*). I can't tell you, Michael, it was… un-fucking-believable. And then suddenly he pulled away from me.

MICHAEL. No!

The loss is palpable… for both of them.

JUSTINE. I know! And he said: 'It's all moot for the time being, anyway.'

MICHAEL. It's all moot?

JUSTINE. Moot, yeah. I know. It's how he talks. I don't think he knows what it sounds like. He says it's all moot cos he's got to go to Hamburg to see the German end for a week, so he'll be missing me like oxygen – 'like oxygen' – he says, and I can just be relieved I've not got him knocking around the office making a fool of himself…

MICHAEL. No?!

JUSTINE. And then he says: 'You never know. You might even miss me when I've gone.' And then it happened…

She looks at him, bereft.

MICHAEL. What?

JUSTINE. I started missing him.

MICHAEL. No!

JUSTINE. Just because the fucker said I would! I thought: *don't go.* I just couldn't *stand* the idea of him leaving!

MICHAEL. You didn't say it?

JUSTINE. No!

MICHAEL. You *didn't.*

JUSTINE. No, of course not. I'm not as big a twat as that.

It's worse:

I said: 'So why not take me with you?'

MICHAEL. No!

JUSTINE. I did! I did!

MICHAEL. I can't believe this! Do you want to go?

JUSTINE. I don't know.

MICHAEL. Then why did you say that?

JUSTINE. I just didn't think. It was just what happened next.

MICHAEL. So what did he say?

JUSTINE. Well, he looked a bit surprised – as though he hadn't thought of it before…

MICHAEL. And…?

JUSTINE. And he said – like this was a very good idea just dawning:

A tone of delicious anticipation – he's definitely going to follow through on this:

'I could. In theory. I suppose I quite easily could.'

MICHAEL. And then…?

JUSTINE *struggles… the horrible truth:*

JUSTINE. And then nothing.

MICHAEL. What d'you mean?

JUSTINE. I mean *nothing*.

MICHAEL. So he didn't like… ask.

JUSTINE. No.

MICHAEL. Fuck. *Fuck.*

JUSTINE. Exactly.

MICHAEL. That's a total disaster.

JUSTINE. I know.

MICHAEL. Fuck.

JUSTINE. I don't know what happened.

MICHAEL. That's a motorway pile-up with a cherry on the top.

JUSTINE. Shit.

MICHAEL. You have just put yourself in an *awful* position.

Transition: the sound of the city – cars, people, sirens, speed.

8.

SADDO *and* MICHAEL.

SADDO *on the phone, very angry.*

MICHAEL *on the other end.*

SADDO. You used the card.

MICHAEL. I know I did. It was an emergency.

SADDO. An emergency?

MICHAEL. Yes.

SADDO. You bought a T-shirt off a website!

MICHAEL. How do you know?

SADDO. Well, how on earth d'you think I know? I checked it out. I called the card people and checked it out.

MICHAEL. I'm sorry.

SADDO. That's a lot of money for a T-shirt too.

MICHAEL. It's a special one.

SADDO. It would have t'be at that price! Whatever possessed you?

MICHAEL. You hadn't called!

SADDO. I'm under no obligation to call.

MICHAEL. It had been a long time. All through Christmas, through New Year… Then I thought: any day now. But *nothing*.

SADDO. I've stopped calling! That's it. End of story!

MICHAEL*'s hanging on the other end.*

God, how dare you…? How *could* you just…?

MICHAEL. I had to do something… t'get your attention… And you gave me the numbers… the MasterCard… I thought maybe you wanted me to.

SADDO. You thought wrong. And I've cancelled the card – the card's dead, it's all cancelled, and I won't be calling again.

MICHAEL. No, wait….

SADDO. Forget it.

But MICHAEL *persists.*

MICHAEL. I'm sorry…

SADDO. It's too late for sorry!

MICHAEL (*bold, accusing*). You missed me!

SADDO. I what…?

MICHAEL. I think you missed me. I think that's true and I want you to say it…

SADDO*'s apparently shocked.*

SADDO. You're deluded. Completely deluded.

MICHAEL. You *missed* me.

SADDO. Look, this isn't *personal*…

This is… It's…

The whole point of this is… There's no… We don't…

Nobody gets hurt. That's the whole point.

SADDO *runs out of words…* MICHAEL *hears…*

MICHAEL. All through Christmas, through New Year, I waited, I missed you….

SADDO*'s running out of anger, too.*

SADDO. You missed my business…

MICHAEL. All through New Year's as well…

SADDO. You've done well out of me...

MICHAEL. Stop it. Don't do that.

SADDO. Well, that's over now – I never intended...

MICHAEL (*softly... as Juliet again*). Please... Daddy...

SADDO. Don't call me that.

MICHAEL. Please... I'll make it up to you.

SADDO. There's no point, it's no use...

MICHAEL. There must be something...

SADDO. Stop this, you're embarrassing yourself...

MICHAEL. No I'm not. How could there be any embarrassment between you and me...? Hm?

SADDO *hears this...*

(*Pushing on, desperate, very persuasive.*) Between you and me, Daddy? No. It's not possible.

SADDO (*quietly concurs*). No...

MICHAEL. Never ever...

The atmosphere settles a little between them.

I'm sorry... I've been a silly girl... But I had to do something to get you to call me. And I'd seen this T-shirt. I look good in this T-shirt, Daddy. You can't imagine.

SADDO*'s giving in, no matter how reluctantly.*

SADDO. This isn't appropriate...

MICHAEL. I ordered the small. I should probably have had the medium. It's a bit tight. Makes it come up short.

SADDO (*without conviction*). Stop...

MICHAEL. Mm-hm. I don't know what you'd think of it. I'm worried about looking... well... slutty...

SADDO. Please... please... that's not how I want it to go...

MICHAEL. I wish you could see it… I'd like your opinion…

We hear SADDO*'s breathing.*

I wonder what you'd think if you could see it…? If I was standing in front of you wearing it now… If I was kneeling down in front of you, right now, wearing just this…?

SADDO. Well… maybe you could send me a photo…

MICHAEL *gasps.*

MICHAEL. A photo?

SADDO. Mm-hm.

MICHAEL. Of me in it?

SADDO. Yes, Juliet. Since I paid for it.

MICHAEL. Okay.

SADDO. But not your face. I don't want to see your face.

MICHAEL. No. No, of course not…

SADDO*'s tone begins to relax back into the old familiarity.*

SADDO. After all, I know what that looks like.

MICHAEL. You do, yes.

SADDO. I know that well enough.

MICHAEL. Yes you do, Daddy.

Beat. A first now for MICHAEL *and* SADDO*:*

I love you, Daddy.

SADDO. I know you do.

MICHAEL. And I'm sorry…

SADDO. That's alright. Good girl. You just got a bit…

MICHAEL. I'll make it up to you.

SADDO. I know you will.

SADDO *considers a moment, then:*

Put my card through.

MICHAEL. I don't care about that.

SADDO. Well, I do. It's a new card, a new set of numbers…

MICHAEL (*pleads*). Later, please… In a minute…

SADDO *allows this.*

I'm kneeling in front of you, Daddy. Where are you?

SADDO *struggles a little, then:*

SADDO. I'm just sitting in the lounge here. I'm watching the birds on the feeder. Your mother put the toast crusts out earlier. It's swamped with them.

MICHAEL. What kind?

SADDO. Well, there's sparrows, a robin… A pigeon keeps trying to get in – it's too big…

MICHAEL. Is Mother home, Daddy?

SADDO. No, it's just me.

MICHAEL. Just the two of us.

SADDO. Yes.

MICHAEL. I like it like this… Just the two of us…

SADDO (*barely audible*). Yes.

MICHAEL. Are you getting hard, Daddy? With me sitting here like this.

SADDO. Yes, I am, princess.

MICHAEL. Oh, I can see. That must be quite uncomfortable. Are you going to unzip it for me? Or would you like me to do it?

SADDO *hesitates a moment.*

SADDO. I'll do it for you.

MICHAEL. Oh, that's so much better... I missed you so badly, Daddy...

SADDO*'s hand slips down the front of his trousers.*

SADDO. The new numbers for the card...

MICHAEL. I missed you so badly...

SADDO. The numbers...

MICHAEL. It's too late for that now.

SADDO. Oh, Juliet...

MICHAEL. Daddy...

SADDO. Oh, Juliet...

MICHAEL. Daddy...

SADDO. You're going to be the death of me...

Lights fade on the sound of both men panting and whimpering... Segue into 'Wannabe' by The Spice Girls.

9.

Lights up on JUSTINE *holding up a T-shirt. It's red and the word 'Love' is scrawled across the front of it in black. She holds it against herself.*

JUSTINE. Hello – dumbstruck!

> MICHAEL*'s here too now.*

MICHAEL. Put it on!

JUSTINE. I love it. God, I only bloody love it!

> *She pulls off the shirt she was wearing earlier, pulls on the red one.*

MICHAEL. Let me see, let me see…

> *It's on now.*

JUSTINE. It's perfect. A bit snug. I could maybe have done with the medium. Still.

> *She looks in the mirror.*

It's perfect.

MICHAEL. Yes, but look at the shirt, really look in the mirror…

> *She does so.*

JUSTINE. It's alright, don't you think? I can not eat for a few days. I can just drink and not eat…

MICHAEL. But look at the shirt…

> JUSTINE *finally does – and she gasps.*

JUSTINE. No!

MICHAEL. Yes!

JUSTINE. I don't… no! No – that just can not be… 'Hate'! It says 'hate'!

MICHAEL. Cos it's reversed, see? The love turns to hate in the mirror. It's the way the letters are designed…

JUSTINE. Oh, that is un-bloody-believable. That is the coolest thing I've ever… Oh my God… How cool is that? How fucking fucking cool… Where would you even get something like this from?

MICHAEL. Please – I spend so much time online…

JUSTINE *is genuinely touched by this.*

JUSTINE. I can't believe you got this for me.

MICHAEL. It's nothing.

JUSTINE. No, I mean it. Cos I sometimes think I come home and I dump all my like crazy bloody shit on you and you're so *good* about it.

I sometimes think I'm not that good a flatmate.

MICHAEL. You're a very good flatmate.

JUSTINE. I'm always storming around going on about how I can't find any knickers.

MICHAEL. I don't mind that.

JUSTINE. And I know I leave hair in the plughole sometimes… I get halfway to work and remember…

MICHAEL. Oh God, those things don't matter. I always think you must get sick of me.

JUSTINE. Why?

MICHAEL. Well, I'm always here. I sometimes think you might like the place to yourself.

JUSTINE. I *never* think that.

MICHAEL. Really?

JUSTINE. Babe. Think how nice it is for me. Knowing you're always here.

She hugs him. He submits to it uncomfortably... Then:

MICHAEL. You look so great in that.

JUSTINE. D'you think?

MICHAEL. Let's get a picture!

JUSTINE. No...

MICHAEL. Yeah, why not? Come on, indulge me...

JUSTINE. I can't... No, I feel stupid...

MICHAEL. Hey – get your light out from under that bushel! You look amazing!

JUSTINE *smiles, touched, almost ready to believe it.* MICHAEL *looks for something.*

JUSTINE. D'you think it's too early to get a bikini wax?

MICHAEL. What?

JUSTINE. He's back from Hamburg on Tuesday, so I want it t'have time t'calm down... just in case...

MICHAEL. Are you thinking it's all going to happen that fast?

He produces a camera.

JUSTINE. I think it might, Michael. I tell you, the sexual tension is unbelievable.

MICHAEL. Okay, let me see some of that!

JUSTINE. Un-fucking-believable. It's since he's not been in the office.

MICHAEL. Come on...

JUSTINE *works a series of comically sexy poses for him.*

JUSTINE. Not seeing each other, it really makes it different. There's that weird intimacy thing when people are a long way away, you know?

MICHAEL. Mm…?

JUSTINE. I mean, he doesn't say much when he calls, he's not the type: 'Hello, beautiful, just checking in…' y'know. He texts a lot.

MICHAEL. Yeah, well, texts are cheap. Free, if you're on the right plan.

JUSTINE. He sent one this morning. You know what it said?

MICHAEL. No.

JUSTINE. 'Hoping everything's under control.' He melts me. He's filthy, but I'm lost. I'm just totally lost. Don't you think I seem calmer?

MICHAEL. You do, yeah… Oh, why not, sweetie? Wax away. Last one –

She poses for one more snap –

Wax lyrical.

He stops photographing, looks at the shots in the back of the camera.

JUSTINE. Let me see…

MICHAEL. I'm not very good…

JUSTINE. Let me look though…

She checks the back of the camera.

Oh God, you're rubbish! Half of these haven't even got my head in!

MICHAEL. I know, I'll delete those.

JUSTINE. This one's alright… God – I'm smiling…

MICHAEL. I'll print that one. We'll have it framed on the side…

JUSTINE. I'm smiling look, Michael. Really smiling. Shit!

MICHAEL. What?

JUSTINE. I don't know… just…

She's amazed to find:

I'm just suddenly really *really* happy.

Music comes up: 'Can't Get You Out of My Head' by Kylie Minogue.

10.

SADDO *and* MICHAEL.

The beginning of a session. A tentative calm between them.

SADDO. Process the card.

MICHAEL. We don't have to do that…

SADDO. I'd prefer to.

MICHAEL. Oh, at least till I've paid you back for the T-shirt…

SADDO. No, put it through.

MICHAEL. In a minute.

(*As Juliet.*) Please, Daddy…

SADDO (*firmly*). I don't want to do that till you've processed the card.

MICHAEL *absorbs this. Returns to his normal voice.*

MICHAEL. Sure. Are you going to tell me the numbers?

SADDO. Not this time. I'll do it on PayPal.

MICHAEL. You don't trust me any more. I don't blame you.

SADDO *won't be drawn.*

I'll put it through.

MICHAEL *types into his computer screen.*

SADDO. Thank you.

MICHAEL. You can key in the numbers now.

SADDO *does so. A moment, then:*

MICHAEL. Your card just cleared.

SADDO *nods.* MICHAEL *waits. Then risks:*

Daddy.

SADDO. Always has, always will. Always kept on top of that.

MICHAEL *transitions comfortably into Juliet.*

MICHAEL. So, did you get the pictures?

SADDO. I did, yes… I've looked at them… a lot…

I've thought of you… a lot…

MICHAEL. Have you…?

MICHAEL *waits.*

You're quiet today, Daddy…

SADDO. I suppose that's right.

I've been thinking.

MICHAEL. About the photos, Daddy?

SADDO. Yes, about the photos.

MICHAEL. Didn't you like them? Didn't you like the shirt, Daddy?

SADDO. Yes, of course I liked them, but…

MICHAEL. There's a thing I haven't told you… about the shirt…

SADDO. Stop…

MICHAEL. There's a thing where you look in the mirror…

SADDO. Would you just listen a minute…? This isn't a game… this is difficult for me…

MICHAEL *stops.*

Juliet…

He struggles.

You wear something like that… you prance around in it… it gives people ideas.

MICHAEL. You don't like it…

SADDO. It's not about whether I like it or not. It's about the effect it has… There are consequences to our actions. When are you going to understand that? When're you going to take some responsibility?

MICHAEL*'s genuinely sorry.*

MICHAEL. I'm sorry, Daddy…

SADDO. This is how trouble gets started.

MICHAEL. Yes, Daddy.

SADDO *presses on.*

SADDO. D'you remember the holiday at Skelmorlie…?

MICHAEL *relocates his 'Juliet'.*

MICHAEL. Of course I do…

He's increasingly secure in the part.

I loved Skelmorlie…

SADDO. The caravan…

MICHAEL. Yes…

SADDO. You got bitten by midges…

MICHAEL. I got eaten alive…

SADDO. I had to put the lotion on. Dab the lotion all over you.

MICHAEL. You took good care of me, Daddy.

SADDO. Yes. Yes, I did.

MICHAEL. Do you want me to take care of you now?

SADDO. I told your mother you should have been more covered up. I said you'd get bitten. She paid no attention. It wasn't her fault, I'm not saying that. But you…

MICHAEL. I was covered… I was itchy…

SADDO. All over.

MICHAEL. I wanted to scratch.

SADDO. I wouldn't let you.

MICHAEL. Don't scratch, you said, it only makes it worse. I couldn't help it, though.

SADDO. I could hear you scraping in the night. Scraping and scratching away in your sleep.

MICHAEL. Scraping and scratching, weals coming up on my skin, Daddy… my little hands, unstoppable…

SADDO. No one could have stood it…

MICHAEL. I know…

SADDO. How your mother slept through it, I'll never…

MICHAEL. She did, though…

SADDO. She did, yes.

MICHAEL. It was just you and me that night.

SADDO. Yes. Yes, while your mother lay sleeping…

MICHAEL. Let me take care of you, Daddy…

SADDO. You can't carry on like this, Juliet.

MICHAEL. Are you going to take your belt off?

SADDO. No. I'm sorry.

We're beyond that now.

MICHAEL. What then…?

SADDO. I'm getting the toolbox from under the stairs.

A chill runs through MICHAEL.

MICHAEL. Why're you doing that, Daddy?

SADDO *shakes his head, pained. He goes off, leaving*
MICHAEL *alone.*

Daddy…?

*An alarm begins to sound, rising to an intolerable pitch,
then:*

11.

The alarm cuts silent. Lights up on JUSTINE, *collapsed on the
sofa, her head hanging off the side. She looks terrible. She's
wearing the 'Love' T-shirt.* MICHAEL'*s exactly where he was
before. He looks hollowed out.*

JUSTINE *stirs a very little.* MICHAEL *notices. The
atmosphere is heavy, everything muted, slowed right down.*

After a moment:

MICHAEL. Can I get you anything?

JUSTINE *scarcely moves, but the answer's no. They
continue in silence for a moment, then:*

JUSTINE. I'm sorry.

MICHAEL. Forget it.

JUSTINE. I set off the burglar alarm.

MICHAEL. Doesn't matter.

JUSTINE. I was sick in your sound-effects bucket.

MICHAEL. No, you weren't.

JUSTINE. I was. I remember.

MICHAEL. Quite near it.

JUSTINE *understands.*

JUSTINE (*scarcely audible*). Oh God…

MICHAEL. It's okay. I cleaned up.

JUSTINE. Michael, I'm so…

MICHAEL. You were very upset.

JUSTINE. I don't know what to say…

MICHAEL. Stop it.

JUSTINE *breathes some more. She's in a truly terrible state.*

JUSTINE. I'll make it up to you.

MICHAEL. No need. Don't worry.

She seems to accept this. Not much choice.

How're you feeling…?

She looks at him. Awful.

I'm sorry.

JUSTINE. Not your fault.

MICHAEL. I know, but still.

JUSTINE *remembers.*

JUSTINE. You were on a call. When I came in. Did I wreck it?

MICHAEL. I was finished.

JUSTINE. You were sitting there, though. With the phone in your hand.

MICHAEL. I was just… you know.

He shrugs.

JUSTINE. Right.

You wouldn't expect me back so early.

MICHAEL. Doesn't matter. Only Saddo.

JUSTINE *absorbs this.*

JUSTINE. What did he want?

MICHAEL *considers a moment... Something different here... Then:*

MICHAEL. He wanted to play a blowtorch on my pussy.

JUSTINE *is struck silent for a moment... Then:*

JUSTINE. Michael...

MICHAEL. Until it was really really charred.

JUSTINE. No...

MICHAEL. And then he wanted to rub in some burns ointment. Very slowly, very gently.

MICHAEL *shrugs.* JUSTINE*'s deeply upset.*

JUSTINE. You can't do this any more.

MICHAEL. I can.

JUSTINE. You can't! *I* can't! Don't tell me you're not upset about that?

MICHAEL. I haven't got a pussy. There's nothing to be upset about.

JUSTINE. Michael...

MICHAEL. No. I don't want to discuss it. Especially not now. With everything.

The subject settles a little between them. JUSTINE *considers a little while, then:*

JUSTINE. Do you ever think about me?

MICHAEL. In what way?

JUSTINE. When you're working.

MICHAEL. When I'm working? Why would I?

JUSTINE. I don't know.

But she pursues this in her head.

MICHAEL. Justine, it's not real. It's *acting*.

JUSTINE. It feels real, though… doesn't it… sometimes?

MICHAEL. That's only feelings. They don't count. No one gets hurt.

JUSTINE. Don't they?

MICHAEL. Not really.

JUSTINE. I feel hurt. Right now.

MICHAEL. But you're not.

JUSTINE. But I *feel* it.

MICHAEL. You're just upset about the other thing. You're too…

JUSTINE. What?

MICHAEL. Well, you let things *get* to you.

JUSTINE *lies back down again.*

You've got to learn to block them out.

Look, maybe it's getting too hard, me doing this here.

JUSTINE. I think it might be.

MICHAEL. Maybe I should look for somewhere else.

JUSTINE*'s caught by surprise.*

JUSTINE. That's not what I meant…

MICHAEL. We always said we'd just see how it went… When I rented the room, after Julie moved out, we said…

JUSTINE. No! Michael… no.

She struggles back up, needs to win him back round.

Look, you were right. I'm just upset about the other thing.

He nods, accepts this. Eventually:

MICHAEL. You want to tell me?

JUSTINE. No.

MICHAEL. Alright.

They sit in silence for a moment, then:

JUSTINE. 'You're looking very svelte.' He said.

MICHAEL *takes this in.*

MICHAEL. Svelte?

JUSTINE. Svelte. As if everything was completely normal.

She shakes her head.

I said: 'Yes, I know, it's this alcohol-only diet. It's fantastic. I've only been on it a fortnight and I've already lost three days.'

The joke sits sad and flat between them.

MICHAEL. Did he laugh?

JUSTINE. No.

MICHAEL. Well, that's something, I s'pose.

JUSTINE (*a genuine enquiry*). Am I stupid?

MICHAEL. No. Of course not.

JUSTINE. I must be.

MICHAEL. You're not.

JUSTINE. Why did I want him?

MICHAEL. I don't know.

JUSTINE. I don't even know who he is.

MICHAEL. You don't want to.

JUSTINE *shakes her head, appalled at the recollection.*

JUSTINE. He took her to lunch. 'It's Alexandra's first day…
I'm taking her down to the Thai place,' he said. I said fine.
'She was a big help out in Hamburg,' he said. 'She speaks
the language, her mother's Swiss. She speaks Italian too.
It's a huge advantage in life having languages,' he said. 'Do
you speak another language, Justine?'

I said French. Bad schoolgirl French.

And I thought he might have the balls to make a joke about
bad schoolgirls. But he didn't.

I went to the pub. I wanted a drink. There was a leaving do
on. Not someone I really know, but the same building. The
graphics place up on the top floor, y'know. There was a
woman there. She was nice to me.

It made me cry.

The emotion resurfaces for a moment. JUSTINE *fights to
collect herself.*

I went back to work.

I was in his office, I was looking around.

The scene fills her head.

MICHAEL. That's when he came in…?

JUSTINE. There's nothing personal. He's like the man who
wasn't there. I was thinking – it's as if he doesn't exist. It's
as if I just made him up. What was I thinking?

MICHAEL. Well, don't think about it any more. Do you think
he's thinking about it? Of course he's not. He's having
dinner with his wife, their friends, in their big house. He's
forgotten it ever happened.

JUSTINE. I didn't hear him come in. He looked surprised. He
said: 'Are you alright, Justine? Have you lost something?'

I said: 'What do you mean, Nigel.' I mean, I knew what he meant but what could I say… I was going through his drawers, y'know?

MICHAEL. Sweetheart…

JUSTINE. 'Have you lost something?'

'No.' I said.

And he just looked at me.

'Look, Nigel… about Alexandra,' I said…

He said: 'I think she'll be an asset on the project.' I said: 'Oh, come off it – we all know you're fucking her!'

He said: 'I beg your pardon?'

MICHAEL. You don't know he's fucking her…

JUSTINE. I said: 'Christ, Nigel, she's twenty-two and she can't spell "Wednesday", why else would you ever have given her a job?' I said: 'She's twenty-two – your daughter's eighteen! What's the fuck's the matter with you? It's just horrible!'

He said: 'I think you had better go home. Go home and cool off.'

She rests in the horror of it for a moment.

I should have come straight home.

Mary Kane saw me on the way out. She said: 'You look ropey.' I said: 'I don't want to talk about it.' She said: 'I saw this coming.'

I went back to the pub. The woman had gone. I stayed a bit anyway. Stayed quite a while.

She struggles to piece together the rest.

I got a cab home, I think. I know I did. The driver wanted to talk. I can't remember what about.

The hopelessness of it all settles heavily on JUSTINE. *She's very very low now.*

Sometimes I don't know what I do all day, Michael. I get home and I'm so tired. It's dark when I go out, it's dark when I get home… and I'm so tired.

MICHAEL. I know.

JUSTINE. 'Have you lost something…?'

MICHAEL. I am sorry.

JUSTINE. Sometimes I feel like I'm holding it all up, all on my own.

MICHAEL. I know.

JUSTINE. I'm so lonely.

MICHAEL. I know.

JUSTINE. And I'm so angry.

MICHAEL. I know.

JUSTINE. And I feel very young sometimes. Like I haven't got a clue. And I feel…

MICHAEL. What?

JUSTINE. Sad. No, not sad. Worse than sad… I feel…

MICHAEL. What?

JUSTINE. Disappointed.

MICHAEL *hears this.*

MICHAEL. Yeah.

He goes over to sit with her.

JUSTINE. And I'm frightened. I'm not even sure what of.

MICHAEL. No.

He holds her.

JUSTINE. I don't even know who you can trust any more…

MICHAEL. No.

JUSTINE. Don't know who you can trust.

MICHAEL. It's alright. It's alright…

JUSTINE. Thank God I've got you. I'd don't know what I'd do if…

MICHAEL. No. Shush… shush, now. Here, look… I've got you…

He holds her.

JUSTINE. So lonely, Michael.

MICHAEL. Yeah, but I've got you now.

A terrible thought crosses JUSTINE*'s mind.*

JUSTINE. Don't leave me.

MICHAEL. Don't be silly. How could I?

JUSTINE. You couldn't, could you? You'd be hopeless.

MICHAEL. That's right.

JUSTINE. You'd be useless without me.

MICHAEL. Of course I would.

He keeps holding her.

JUSTINE. You won't leave me…?

MICHAEL. *Would* I…?

JUSTINE. Michael…?

MICHAEL *tightens his grip, rocks* JUSTINE.

MICHAEL. Shush now… Shush now.

The barest hesitation before:

Would I…?

The question hangs in the air as the lights fade to black…

The End.

A Nick Hern Book

Herding Cats first published in Great Britain in 2011 as a paperback original by Nick Hern Books Limited, The Glasshouse, 49a Goldhawk Road, London W12 8QP, in association with David Luff Productions

Reprinted 2012

Herding Cats copyright © 2011 Lucinda Coxon

Lucinda Coxon has asserted her right to be identified as the author of this work

Cover photograph: Simon Annand
Cover design: Ned Hoste, 2H

Typeset by Nick Hern Books, London
Printed in the UK by Mimeo Ltd, Huntingdon, Cambridgeshire PE29 6XX

A CIP catalogue record for this book is available from the British Library

ISBN 978 1 84842 240 7